POP CULTURE BIOS
SUPER SINGERS

TAYLOR
SWIFT

COUNTRY POP HIT MAKER

ROBIN NELSON

Lerner Publications Company
MINNEAPOLIS

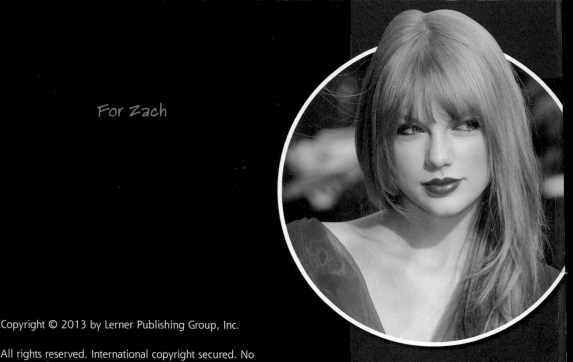

For Zach

Lerner Publications Company
A division of Lerner Publishing Group, Inc.
241 First Avenue North
Minneapolis, MN 55401 U.S.A.

Website address: www.lernerbooks.com

Library of Congress Cataloging-in-Publication Data

Nelson, Robin, 1971–
    Taylor Swift : country pop hit maker / by Robin Nelson.
        p.   cm. — (Pop culture bios. Super singers)
    Includes index.
    ISBN 978–0–7613–4143–7 (lib. bdg. : alk. paper)
    1. Swift, Taylor, 1989– 2. Women country musicians—United States—Biography—Juvenile literature. I. Title.
    ML3930.S989N45 2013
    782.421642092—dc23 [B]   2011052631

Manufactured in the United States of America
1 – PC – 7/15/12

INTRODUCTION

The night of November 7, 2007, was huge for Taylor Swift. She was at the Country Music Association (CMA) Awards. She'd been nominated for the Horizon Award. This award honors the up-and-coming country artist of the year. She'd grown up watching other artists win this award. And here she was, seventeen years old and nominated herself!

Taylor spent tons of time primping for the awards show. She got her hair and makeup done. She picked out a beautiful gold gown. As she walked the red carpet, she posed for pics. She waved to fans. She was having a blast!

Taylor's glam look wowed fans waiting on the red carpet for the CMA Awards in 2007.

Taylor rocks the stage at the 2007 CMAs.

During the show, Taylor got to perform. She swapped out her gown for a sparkly black dress. Playing her crystal-encrusted guitar—Taylor *loves* sparkles!—she sang "Our Song" to a room packed with country music celebs.

Then it was time to announce the Horizon Award winner. Taylor was back in her gown and sitting in the audience. She was crazy with nerves as last year's winner, country singer and *American Idol* champ Carrie Underwood, read the nominees. Carrie finally opened the envelope and said, "And the Horizon Award goes to... Taylor Swift!"

Taylor could hardly believe it! She hurried onstage. **"I want to thank my family for moving to Nashville so that I could do this,"** she gushed. **"And the fans, you have changed my life. This is definitely the highlight of my senior year."**

Taylor would go on to score many other awards in the future. But this award at the CMAs meant she had arrived on the music scene. The starlet's biggest dreams were coming true.

Taylor was ecstatic during her acceptance speech for the Horizon Award.

CHAPTER ONE

LITTLE GIRL WITH A BIG IMAGINATION

Taylor with her mom, Andrea, and her brother, Austin

Taylor and her dad, Scott

Taylor Alison Swift was born on December 13, 1989. Her dad, Scott, is a stockbroker. He helps people manage their money. Her mom, Andrea, quit her job in business to be a stay-at-home mom. A couple years later, Taylor's brother, Austin, was born.

Taylor and her brother spent their early childhood on their family's Christmas tree farm in Wyomissing, Pennsylvania. Taylor had to help on the farm by pulling bugs off the trees. *Eeew!* Taylor and Austin had a lot of space to play. Taylor loved using her imagination to make up stories and act them out on the farm.

Taylor at the age of four

Born to Sing

Taylor started singing when she was very young. Her mom sang nursery rhymes with her. Andrea noticed that Taylor had an awesome voice. Sometimes Taylor even changed the words. Her mom thought this was cute. She didn't know that it was just the beginning of Taylor's songwriting career!

When she was older, Taylor loved writing stories and poems. She tried to find the perfect words to tell a story. She won a national poetry contest when she was in fourth grade. Her poem was called "Monster in My Closet."

IT'S IN THE STARS

Taylor's zodiac sign is Sagittarius. But is Taylor really a Sagittarius girl? Totes! These Sag traits describe Taylor to a T:

positive
fun
enthusiastic
generous
honest

confident
ambitious
adventurous
independent

Taylor also loved being in school plays. At one point, she played a guy and wore a fake mustache. She really wanted the part because it was the only one that sang a solo.

Taylor's favorite thing about being in plays was the parties afterward. There she sang karaoke. She loved listening to country music, so she sang country songs. Soon Taylor started entering karaoke contests. She sounded awesome (no surprises there!), and she kept perfecting her act until she went home with a prize.

KARAOKE =
singing the lyrics to a
song while a machine plays
the instrumental part

Taylor loves to sing!
She's been singing since
she was really young.

CHAPTER TWO

ON TO NASHVILLE

Music Row in Nashville, Tennessee

Singing karaoke made Taylor decide she wanted to be a professional country singer. She knew she needed a demo CD. She recorded herself singing her karaoke songs. Taylor also knew she needed to go to Nashville, Tennessee. Nashville is the heart of country music. Most of the country music recording companies are there. So when she was ten, she started hitting up her parents to take her to Nashville. She begged them every single day!

Taylor's parents finally caved when she was eleven. They took Taylor to

DEMO CD =
a CD that musicians make to show how their music sounds

Nashville over her spring break. Taylor's mom drove her down Music Row. It's a street filled with country music companies. Taylor jumped out of the car at each one. She went in and left one of her demo CDs. But none of the companies called her.

Taylor decided she needed to be different to stand out from other singers. She needed to work on her own music. Taylor learned to play guitar when she was twelve. Then she wrote her first song.

At school, things weren't going so well for Taylor. In fact, they were pretty awful. Her classmates didn't get why she wanted to sing instead of going to sleepovers. They bullied her. Taylor would sit at a lunch table filled with girls, and the girls would get up and leave. Her feelings were hurt a lot. But writing about her feelings helped. "Those girls could say anything they wanted about me," she remembers, "because after school I was going to go home and write a song about it."

A Big Break

Taylor and her mom started going to Nashville every couple of months. They met with songwriters and played them Taylor's songs. They hoped the songwriters could help Taylor get discovered. Soon she had a meeting with the largest music company in Nashville. She sang all her songs for people from RCA Records. They offered her a development deal.

DEVELOPMENT DEAL =

an agreement by a music company to help a singer develop his or her talent. If the artist's talent matures enough, the company gives the artist a recording contract.

A New Home and Life

Taylor's family decided that if her dreams were going to come true, they needed to move to Tennessee. They packed up and moved to Hendersonville, a town just minutes from Nashville. Taylor's dad had to find a new job. Her brother had to make new friends. Taylor knows how much her family has done to help her career. "It was an incredible sacrifice for my parents to make," she said to *CMT Insider.* **"I've never forgotten it."** In 2004 Taylor's development deal with RCA was up. But the company wasn't ready to give her a contract. They wanted her to try singing other people's songs instead of her own.

Taylor and her mom, Andrea

They wanted to make another development deal. Taylor said no. She wanted to sing her own songs. She didn't want to wait for a recording contract. She decided to find a different recording company.

Finding a new company wasn't easy. But Taylor was determined. She sang for companies all over Nashville. Her work finally paid off. Taylor got a songwriting job with Sony/ATV Music in 2005. She wouldn't get to sing the songs she wrote. But she would get to create music. She was fourteen years old and the youngest songwriter ever at the company.

Taylor had to work hard to balance her job with the rest of her life. Every day she went to school. Then her mom picked her up and took her to Nashville. She worked with other songwriters on songs for other people. Then she went home to eat dinner and do homework.

Taylor's social life was better in Tennessee. The kids at school were supportive of her dreams. She made tons of friends. Taylor was happier. She was getting As in school. She was earning her own money. And she sang at cafés and nightclubs on the weekends.

A New Deal

One night Taylor was singing her songs at a Nashville café. A man named Scott Borchetta was in the audience. He loved Taylor's singing and her songs. Borchetta was starting his own music company. He wanted to sign a contract with Taylor. He wanted Taylor to sing her own songs. It was Taylor's dream shot! At fifteen, she became the first artist to sign a contract with Borchetta's new company, Big Machine Records.

Taylor poses with Scott Borchetta at a Nashville event in 2011.

17

CHAPTER THREE

BECOMING A STAR

The first single Taylor recorded was called "Tim McGraw." She thought of the idea for the song when she was in her ninth-grade math class. The words and melody were in her head, and she didn't want to forget them. So she asked her teacher if she could go to the bathroom. In the bathroom, she recorded herself singing part of the song into her phone. "Tim McGraw" was released in 2006 when Taylor was sixteen. It crept up the country music charts and eventually made it to number six.

SINGLE =

one song. Sometimes a single is sold as part of an album. Other times, a single is sold all by itself.

WHO IS TIM MCGRAW?

Tim McGraw (*LEFT*) is a country singer. Taylor's song "Tim McGraw" is about a girl whose boyfriend is going away to college. The girl hopes her BF will think of her every time he hears a song by Tim McGraw.

Taylor's first album, *Taylor Swift*, was released in October 2006. She was super scared about what people would think of it. But Taylor didn't need to worry. Fans *adored* the recording! It sold thirty-nine thousand copies in its first week.

Fans loved that Taylor's songs were about her own life. Listeners of all ages could relate to her feelings about love and heartbreak. **"I like to write songs about boys,"** Taylor spilled in an E! special. "I like to write songs about relationships. It's really, really fun for me to tell stories that have actually happened."

Taylor's second single was very personal. The song was called "Teardrops on My Guitar," and it was about a boy she'd crushed on a couple years ago. His name was Drew, and she used his real name in the song. But Drew liked a different girl then. When the song came out, Drew went to visit Taylor. Now he was into her! But he was too late. Taylor didn't want to date him anymore. But the song made it to number two on the country charts and even made the *Billboard* Top 40.

Crossover Sensation

The *Billboard* Top 40 included all kinds of music, but it mostly featured pop. It was hard for country singers to make it onto the list. But Taylor had made it. In February 2008, Taylor appeared on MTV. MTV didn't usually feature country artists. They called Taylor a crossover sensation—an artist who appeals to both country and pop fans. Taylor had made country music cool even among people who didn't normally like country!

TEAM POP VS. TEAM COUNTRY

Are you on Team Pop or Team Country? Or do you like both these musical styles? There's lots to love about both pop and country. What are the differences between the two?

POP MUSIC (short for "popular music") is a type of music that started in the 1950s. It is upbeat, catchy, and repetitive. You can hear drums, electric guitars, keyboards, and bass in pop music.

COUNTRY MUSIC started in the 1920s. It first came from the southern part of the United States. Country songs often tell stories with strong emotion. Guitars, fiddles, and banjos are popular instruments in country.

CHAPTER FOUR
MEGASTAR

In fall 2008, Taylor released her second album, *Fearless*. It shot to number one on the charts and sold six hundred thousand copies in the first week!

After *Fearless* was released, Taylor spilled a huge secret—she'd had a romance with pop star Joe Jonas of the Jonas Brothers. The couple had kept their relationship under wraps so the media wouldn't dish about them. The romance had inspired the song "Forever & Always" on the *Fearless* album. But the couple was no longer a couple by the time the album came out. Taylor and Joe had broken it off.

Joe Jonas

BF-INSPIRED SONGS

Boys beware! If you date Taylor Swift, she will probably write a song about you. Here are a few former Taylor Swift BFs and the songs that they inspired:

- Joe Jonas, "Forever & Always"
- Taylor Lautner, "Back to December"
- John Mayer, "Dear John"

Taylor Lautner

John Mayer

Fearless and Forgiving

Taylor spent much of 2009 on tour for *Fearless*. She traveled all over the country performing in her own headlining tour.

HEADLINING TOUR = a tour in which one artist is the main act. An artist with his or her own headlining tour is the star of the show.

That summer, Taylor's video for "You Belong with Me" was nominated for an MTV Video Music Award. Taylor was thrilled to have her work nominated alongside that of Beyoncé and Lady Gaga. Even better, at the ceremony in September, Taylor's video won! She was the first country singer ever to win a Video Music Award.

The awards were notable for another reason too. When Taylor got onstage to speak after scoring the award, rapper Kanye West ran up and grabbed the microphone from her! He said he thought Beyoncé had one of the best videos of all time. He suggested that Beyoncé should have won instead of Taylor. Taylor was visibly shaken. When Kanye left the stage, she couldn't even finish her speech.

Later in the evening, Beyoncé did win an award. She won Video of the Year. Beyoncé felt bad that Taylor had been interrupted. So instead of giving a speech herself, she called Taylor back onstage so she could finish her speech. Kanye later called Taylor to apologize, and Taylor readily forgave him. About her convo with Kanye, Taylor spilled, **"I think that you learn a lot of lessons as you're growing up, and one of them has to be human compassion."**

Taylor gives her speech at the 2009 MTV Video Music Awards.

Have you ever seen a pic of Taylor with the number thirteen drawn on her right hand? She never takes the stage without adorning her hand with that number. Why? It's because she considers thirteen lucky! She was born on December 13. She turned thirteen on Friday the thirteenth. Her first number one song had a thirteen-second intro. To Taylor, the number thirteen represents awesome things.

More Big Wins

At the CMA Awards that year, Taylor scored five awards, including Entertainer of the Year. In January 2010, she won four—count them, *four!*—Grammy Awards, including Album of the Year for *Fearless*.

In October 2010, Taylor released her third album called *Speak Now*. The album sold more than one million copies in the first week.

On Tour with Taylor

In 2011 Taylor kicked off her *Speak Now* World Tour— her first concert tour around the world. Every one of her concerts sold out in less than five minutes! Early in 2012, she also took home Grammys for Best Country Solo Performance and Best Country Song for "Mean," her megahit from *Speak Now*.

But even with all of her awards and fame, her fans were still the most important thing to her. Before each concert on her world tour, Taylor spent time meeting her fans. Halfway through each concert, she walked through the crowd to sing songs to the people sitting in the back.

Taylor knows she's a role model. She doesn't get into trouble, and she lives her life knowing her fans are watching her. In November 2011, she dished to TV's *60 Minutes* about the responsibility she thinks celebs have to their fans. "Every singer out there with songs on the radio is raising the next generation," she said. **"So make your words count!"**

With Taylor's upbeat attitude and dazzling songwriting skills, there's no doubt that we haven't heard the last from this country songstress. "I've always loved people, and I've always loved creating things," Taylor said in an E! special. **"So when you get to create things and then play it for people…it's the coolest job ever."**

Taylor loves her fans. During concerts she often shakes hands with people in the crowd.

TAYLOR

PICS!

SOURCE NOTES

7   Taylor Swift, "Taylor Swift Wins the CMA Horizon Award," YouTube, posted by laurenmileycyrus, November 11, 2007, http://www.youtube.com/watch?v=NdSmZodCQtQ (December 10, 2011).

14   Amy Gail Hansen, *Taylor Swift: Love Story* (Chicago: Triumph Books, 2009), 17.

15   Taylor Swift, "Teen Star Talks about Her Early Need to Move to Nashville," interview, part 1, *CMT Insider,* November 26, 2008, http://www.cmt.com/news/country-music/1600309/cmt-insider-interview-taylor-swift-part-1-of-2.jhtml (December 18, 2011).

20   E! Entertainment special, "Taylor Swift," E! Entertainment Television, December 1, 2010.

25   Taylor Swift, "You Belong with Me," *New Yorker* 87, no. 31 (October 10, 2011): 104–115.

27   *60 Minutes,* "Taylor Swift: A Young Singer's Meteoric Rise," *CBS News,* November 20, 2011.

27   E!, "Taylor Swift."

MORE TAYLOR INFO

Burlingame, Jeff. *Taylor Swift: Music Superstar.* Berkeley Heights, NJ: Enslow Publishers, 2011.
This fun-to-read book offers readers juicy quotes, personal stories, and features such as a timeline and a glossary.

Cefrey, Holly. *Taylor Swift.* New York: Rosen Central, 2011.
Read all about the life and career of this talented young woman who has become an inspiration to millions of fans.

Facebook: Taylor Swift
http://www.facebook.com/TaylorSwift
Get all the latest Taylor news on her official FB page.

Landau, Elaine. *Beyoncé: R & B Superstar.* Minneapolis: Lerner Publications Company, 2013.
Get the inside scoop on Beyoncé, the artist who gracefully stepped aside at the 2009 MTV Video Music Awards to let Taylor give a speech.

Sachs, Lloyd. *American Country Music: Bluegrass, Honky-Tonk, and Crossover Sounds.* Minneapolis: Twenty-First Century Books, 2013.
If you're a country fan, you'll love this fun and in-depth look at country music.

Taylor Swift
http://www.taylorswift.com
Check out Taylor's official website for updates, photos, videos, and messages from Taylor herself.

INDEX

PHOTO ACKNOWLEDGMENTS

The images in this book are used with the permission of: © Ray Tamarra/Getty Images, pp. 2, 22 (top right); © A. Messerschmidt/Getty Images, pp. 3 (top), 20; © Jason Kempin/Getty Images, pp. 3 (bottom), 28 (right); Stephen Fernandez/Splash News/Newscom, pp. 4 (top left), 4 (top right), 29 (top left); AP Photo/Matt Sayles, p. 4 (bottom); © Michael Loccisano/FilmMagic/Getty Images, p. 5; © Rick Diamond/WireImage/Getty Images, pp. 6, 15, 18 (right); AP Photo/Mark Humphrey, pp. 7, 18 (bottom left); © Rick Diamond/Getty Images for CMT, pp. 8 (bottom left), 19; Randi Radcliff/AdMedia/Newscom, p. 8 (right); © Andrew Orth/Retna Ltd./CORBIS, p. 9; Kristin Callahan/Everett Collection/Newscom, p. 10; ZUMAPress/Newscom, pp. 11, 12 (top); © Andalucia Plus Image Bank/Alamy, p. 12 (bottom); David Mills/Splash News/Newscom, p. 16; © Rick Diamond/Getty Images for ACM, p. 17; © John Shearer/WireImage/Getty Images, p. 18 (top left); © Jeff Kravitz/FilmMagic, Inc/Getty Images, pp. 21, 25; Ahmad Elatab/Splash News/Newscom, p. 22 (top left); AP Photo/Nati Harnik, p. 22 (bottom); © Featureflash/Dreamstime.com, pp. 23 (top), 29 (top middle); © Carrienelson1/Dreamstime.com, pp. 23 (middle), p. 29 (right); © Sbukley/Dreamstime.com, p. 23 (bottom); © Chad Batka/CORBIS, p. 24; © Frederick Breedon IV/Getty Images, p. 26; © Kevin Mazur/WireImage/Getty Images, p. 27; © Keith Bedford/Starbucks via Getty Images, p. 28 (top left); AP Photo/Charles Sykes, p. 28 (bottom left); © Wanderlust/Dreamstime.com, p. 29 (bottom left).

Front cover: © Rob Verhorst/Redferns/Getty Images (left); © D Dipasupil/FilmMagic/Getty Images (right); Back cover: © Ray Tamarra/Getty Images.

Main body text set in Shannon Std Book 12/18.
Typeface provided by Monotype Typography.